P.S. I HATE IT HERE!

P.S. I HATE IT HERE!

KIDS' LETTERS FROM CAMP

Selected and edited by Diane Falanga

Abrams Image
New York

Contents

Foreword

By Diane Falanga

The idea of collecting hilarious letters that kids wrote home from overnight camp came to me a few years ago when I received my first letter from my daughter, Bianca. She was just eight years old and my husband, Mark, our older son, Blake, and I all thought she was too young to go away from home. But Bianca was determined: She begged, pleaded, and assured us that homesickness only affected *seven*-year-olds. She was so confident, we agreed. We packed up her pint-sized duffle bag and sent her off to camp for a week.

Then the first letter arrived.

"I cried because I got homesick . . . they made me clean the table. I want to go HOME."

(Different day. Same letter. As if things couldn't get any worse.)

"I stopped crying . . . But we have chores today. I am the Scraper, Sweeper and Maid."

Maybe I should have called the camp to check on the well-being of my Little Orphan Annie. Instead, I called my sister and girlfriends to read them the letter. Of course I cared about Bianca's happiness at camp, but the guilty pleasure of delivering these quotes—with just the right note of comedic timing—was impossible to resist.

Instantly, friends began to read me their own kids' camp letters and each was more outrageous than the last. The idea of a collection of camp letters was born! After sending out dozens of e-mails and contacting camps around the country, I was able to gather a few hundred more laugh-out-loud gems, contained in *P.S. I Hate It Here*.

These letters reveal that kids are wittier, more complex, and more sophisticated than we assume they'd be at a young age. Ten-year-old Sam wrote, *"One kid is playing other kids for $50 in poker. One kid lost $10. But don't worry, I didn't play. If I did, I would play the house. P.S. Dad, that poker set could have been useful after all."*

The letters also show that when writing from the heart (or when forced by a camp counselor in order to get supper) kids are inadvertently hilarious: *"Dear Mom, Day 5 of camp is a lot better. The rash on my P-nus is gone and now I can run. My friends hate when I say eggs, so I'm trying to stop saying it. Love, Josh."*

This book is not a reflection on camp experiences by adults, but a collection of actual camp letters written home by kids— most getting a taste of independence for the very first time. There's a purity and directness to these letters, which makes them all the more comical and poignant. And while some campers may bitterly complain about hardships and homesickness, they seem to move past these issues instantly, leaving parents at home to fret and anxiously await the next letter. (Or to simply laugh and call their friends.)

Enjoy this hysterical portal into the hearts and minds of kids spending the summer away at camp and this trip down memory lane for so many who remember these days well.

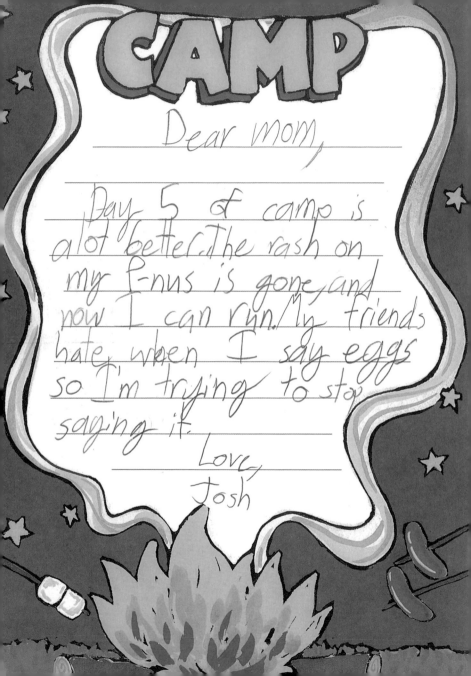

CAMP NEWS

To: _Mom,_

I have a mouse named
ed and a chipmunk
named herman! I love
you and I'm seein' you
in 4 days!!! My toilet
never works! ☹ I miss
you! I met 5 new friends

From: _Rian_

J & L Confetti Corp.

Hi Ted,

Our cabin is really weird. We have a kid who always hides everyones stuff. The bathroom is called "the kybo" which stands for "keep your bowels open." Yesterday we played basketball and wom. Did your team win the playoffs? If not who won?

See ya,

Blake

Dear Mom and Dad it was
nice being able to talk
to you on the phone
exept it got me a little
homesick im trying
to work on my penminship
I hope it is better
I wonder how anna
will like camp

Love zack,

Dear Mom & Dad & Katie,

Right now our cabin and Cornell cabin are in WAR. We are in War because they messed up our entire cabin so we are going to tepi their cabin and put their beds on the ceiling. But enough about me, I want to hear from you. How's the dog, how's Katie, how's the flowers. Well I Love you all.

Sammy

Dear Mom,

We got a chance to hang out with our camp sisters. If you got my message before I'm not a big fan of mine. She is so much older than me 1. She copys me 2. She spits in your face when she talks 3. And four, she was coughing and sneezing in my face Plees whenever she isnt talking (spiting) she was sniffling!! (listen to how gross this is, sometimes it even got in my mouth when she spit!) I'm kind of scared to let her see me!!

From a very very very sad,
Rose

A ^ginormus tree hit our cabin
and knoked it down!
When I was in it! No
one got hurt, though.
It was so scary!
When the roof fell
off our cabin every
thing got soked!
The cleaning people took
all our stuff and dryed
it in a dryer. Now our
cabin sleeps in the
basement of the
health lodge. EWWW!
Please read this
note to Mom.
          LOVE, Juliet

P.S. please do not
be ~~storm~~ alarmed.

Dear Fam,
Hi! Hows every-
thing? Any changes
in the house? Any-
new things happening
to shane? Hows
zach and you guys?
Hows the backyard
looking? any new
changes? Any new
Floats for the
pool? well, hope
you write

*CAMP NEWS *★ ★

Dear   mom and dad

Today was consler

elimpiy it was so

much fun Also i got

gue   on my head

love David ★

Dear mom (and dad)
I got your letter(s).
I am so exited for
you to visit. I
decided that since
you were coming
all the way over
here for the play
that I should be
in the play. So
I'm going to try
to be in the play.
They probably they
probable will let
me be in the
play. I'm actually

I am glad that
you told me about
flippers. Not because
I wanted flippers
to die, it was because
I was happy that
you told me right
away! I still am
pretty sad. So any
way I will try to
be in the play. I will
write back about
it.
    Love,
    Anna/Linnea

Dear mom yesterday
we had a egg drop
contest we came in
first for are egedrop
and seond for the
hole thing also pleas
dont write alot.

xoxo ♥ Kayl

Saturday, June 18

Dear Mom,

Sorry for the wait to get a letter from me. I got the note you wrote me when I left but I wanted to wait until a few days went by and ~~there~~ there were things to talk about. I haven't gotten ~~kiss~~ my pillow yet if you have sent it, but I was able to borrow one from the office. Today there was a chipmunk in our ~~koogee~~ and it ran less than ~~the~~ half a foot in front of me and stopped ~~for~~ for a second and looked up a me befor running under a bed. Also, sorry I waited a day before sending this letter but I wanted to send the letter I wrote to & dad at the same time. Finally, I apogice for writing this letter completly in past tense (like the part were I said my letter was going to be a day late) but I wrote this letter antisipating I would wait a day.

                                        - Henry

Sunday, July 3rd

Dear Mom,

    Thanks for the postcard & Robbie's address.
I sent him a letter, but I think I might get
home either the day arrives or a day before because I
forgot to send it for two days due to lack of envelopes.
~~When~~ It's fine though. Anyway, I have been getting a few
letters from Mama Lores and Anne-Linnea. Anne says
she is having fun and I have been writing back. Mama
Lores wrote saying she enjoyed her visit with us
and she sent me the Sunday comics. Can you
remind me to call her when I get back? To awnser
some questions from your post card: 1. I already had
my dark glasses but thankes for asking. And, 2. ~~here~~
here are my awnsers for the spelling list:

    <u>anticipating</u> - Awaiting or look forwards for.

    <u>routine</u> — A cronic or repetitive pattern, order,
    or schedule.

How was that? I hope I got at least one right.
See you soon.

                    —Henry

Dear Dad,
STOP telling
me about all
the good things
you gues are doing. like
the boat going to their
house for dinner or
the first block party!
you made me very angry!
Love,
your mad daughter

24

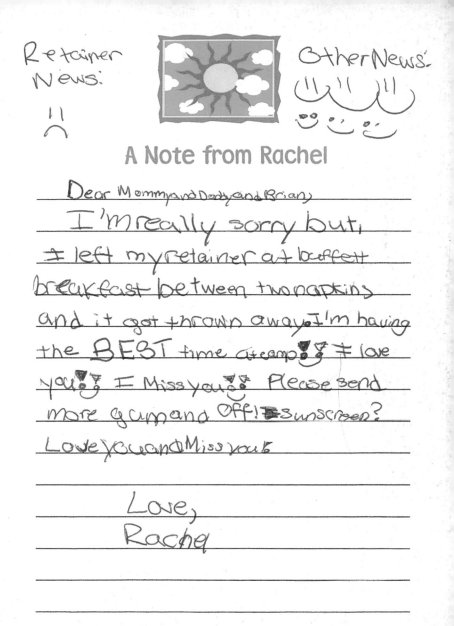

A Note from Rachel

Dear Mommy and Daddy and Brian,

I'm really sorry but,
I left my retainer at buffett
breakfast between two napkins
and it got thrown away. I'm having
the BEST time at camp! I love
you! I Miss you! Please send
more gum and OFF! Sunscreen?
Love you and Miss you

Love,
Rachel

Dear, Mom Dad, Terri, Uncle Allan, and Buffy How are you? I am fine - ~~xxxxxxxxxxx~~ In my supper letter I wrote a little of what I'm going to tell you in this letter. Monday night a policeman came and told Mr Seeger that they spotted a u f o (which means unidentifying flying object. When are cabin found out what happened some people started to cry - (including me). Larraine said if it came any closer that we would have to go to the Mess hall. Larraine

over -

came and told us that we had to go to the Mess hall. As we were going it landed. (It was a space ship). It told us not to be afraid. But I was still crying. Don't be scared it wasn't real. The consulars made it out of a car and lights. (It looked real).

Love,
Deb

27

Nick's News from Camp!

Dear __Mom and Dad__,   Date __7/2/07__

Today I had another fabulous day at Camp Hayo-Went-Ha!

The weather is:

__Good so ~~so~~ far it's cold in the ~~mornings~~.__
__mornings and sometimes at night,__

My favorite activity is:

__So far it is camoflauge, camoflauge is where you hide__
__aint ~~is~~ basically someone needs to find you,__

I love eating __Breakfast__ (favorite meal here). ~~I also like to eat.~~
__So far my favorite meal ~~is~~ was a danish, danish's are pastries__
__with jelly in them, I also ~~~~ like to eat ~~fruit~~ loops.__

My counselor is cool because:

__I have two counselors, ~~one~~ one is from New Zealand,__
__the other is from Holland, Michigan. There names are Mattand__
                                                      __Justin,__

My cabin mates are a great bunch of guys. One of them in particular has a special talent. He can:

__one person can poe there shoulder it's really cool__

_____

I love it here. I may never come home. (fill in more items of interest here):

__My cabin number is 8, and ~~~~ ~~~~ ~~~~ there's mice,__
__some times in your sleeping bag,__

(**Love** / From (please circle one),

__Nicholas__

Your Son / Grandson / Brother / Friend
(please circle one)

Dear Charlie,

(What's up) the answer to your previous question is yes, I do take waterskiing. I can also stand up on a kneeboard.

Dear mom + dad,

How are you doing? Also don't tell Kayla or Charlie but what does the word googly mean because someone called me it, they said it was a swear.

P.S.
I can't wait
to go on the dig!

CAMP

Dear Mom, Dad,

I got Harry Potter. It's amazing, everyone dies. Just kidding. I haven't finished it yet. Thanks for the Hulk comics, they're awesome. Thanks also for the goggles even though the mask is huge. Camp is great. It's hot as hell here. I think I've gained weight here in fact. The food sucks, but I still eat it.

Adios, Mikey

Dear Mom

Yesterday I was sick, but now I am
better. thank you for the brownieze they
were really good. Jack keeps on telling
every camper that I cant read. The
dogs are trouble halfy. The mountin biking
tratls are fun and hard. I hade a bad
fall. I went down a hill and couldent stop
and hit a tree. The mountin bikes are
very good. Bye a have to leave.

Love Nick

Dear Mom & Dad,

Camp is awsome we are all making cool things out of Duct tape but I dont have any. If it isn't any trouble our cabin could use two rolls of the tape. If you decide to send the tape please send it A.S.A.P.

P.S.
How are the fish?

Sam

Dear Mom, Dad, & Charlie,
I miss you a lot
and can't wait to see
you. How are the fish?
P.S.
I miss TV
— Sam

Dear Charlie,

I am really sorry about the fish that died. I only have 4 days left of ~~camp~~ camp.

Love you,

Sam

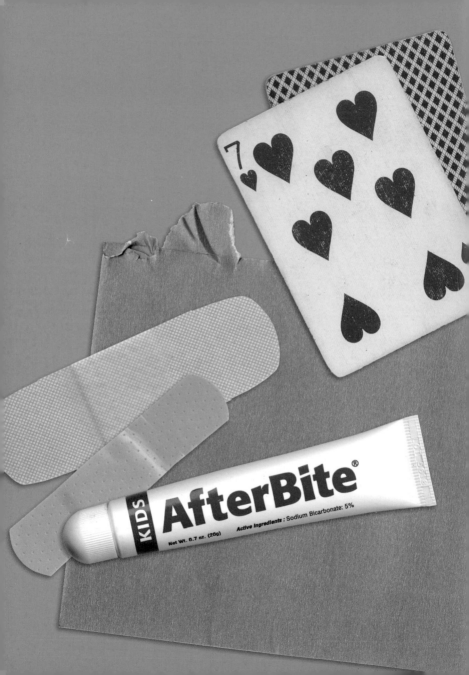

Camp
Ailments

Dear mom and Dad,

I have a <u>really</u> really
<u>REALLY</u> <u>BAD</u> ingrone toenail it
is killing me when we get home get
a doctors apointment PLEASE

          Lots of Love,
           Piper

P.S. see you @ play!!

P.S.S <u>DON'T</u> sign me up for
next year!

Dear, Dad, Mom, and Samantha today I got a rock in my hand I didn't cry I but got the rock out with tweesers. And also today my nose also started bleding to gargle I had salt water because my throwt n eart. What did you do Sunday?

Love, Nichi

xoxoxo

June 22, 2008

Dear Family,

I've had the worst day today!
first I went fishing for 2½ hours.
I didn't even catch one fish!
not one! The I fell down the steps.
I got a cut on my knee, a
bruse on my shin, a cut on
my foot, and 2 cuts on my other shin.
OWCH!!!... Otherwise I am
having fun, though. I can't wait for
the butterscotch carrot cookies!

Love,

Juliet

P.S.
I made the
envalope
myself!

40

Dear mom and dad this will be my
last letter. Today it is 100°f and it is packing
day. So we have to sit around in our
burning hot cabin all day packing we
can't do our activities it is so hot!
Yesturday it was rally day 7 people
asked me to dance. The counslers
want us to wear our fancy outfits
on the plane and we have no choice
so I am going to wear my normal
clothes under my fancy clothes and
change at the airport. We can't take
a shower because we don't have our stuff
so I ran through the sprinkler. Our

Counseler Viki, if she sees you
with a beach ball she'll cut it up. I ♡
ΛΟΛΟΧΟΧΟΧΟΧΟ from: Abigail

our cabin
↙

me swimming
↓

Dear Mom and dad, I think this is the worst year I'll ever have at camp. In horse back riding we never have enough time to acually ride the horse. In archery no ~~one~~ one gets a turn because there is so many ~~people~~ people. In gymnastics I keep on hertig myself I got a huge bruse today. on the up side katie is in my first 2 activities archery and gymnastics. In

water arobics they put me in the younger ~~to~~ group because I am short. So now I am learning how to do the strokes. And dad I'm doing fishing next week

from: abigail

☐=red
▨=green

Dear Family,

Today we went on the pamper pole. It is a huge, wobbely telephone pole that you climb to the top of and jump off. Also my finger got sraiched under a canoe, swelled extra huge, then turned green. Zack the Health guy put acid on it. I exploded with puss. He lifted up my skin and I could see my muscle in my finger. Now it's fine. Also we canoed down the sturgeon River. Thrills.

Mighty sturgeone river / me stealing / David paddling / Quinn

Love,
Dylan

43

Dear Mom and Dad,   July, 4, 2008
I'm ~~too~~ having fun at camp. I signed up for a canoe trip down Moose River. It should be renamed Moos-quito river. The bugs were awful. There were also some rapids on the trip, they were tough. We capsized a canoe and tacoed another.

missing you!

Love,

Mason

8/15/06

Dear Mom + Dad,

Mitch is sick. I saw him at lunch today because its Shabbat. He looks terrible - pale + tired. He told me he had been sleeping at the Health Center for 2 hours but woke up + decided to go to ~~s~~ lunch. He has to go to the Health Center at 7pm. for sick call or a check-up by a doctor. He also told me to write you b/c he's ~~too~~ tired.

My throat has been hurting but I went to the Health Center + its not red or anything. I gargled some salt water.

I also have a rash + the nurse said its probably heat rash so I'm putting aloe on it. I'm fine though + having a great time.

Dear Jess
How do you like the
card Mom picked it
out. It was going to be
for my birthday. My
birth day is in two
days. Sorry I didn't
write you much, I just
had some pawer ade,
It went down the wrong
tube and I coughed
it up it took a lot of napkins
to chean it up,

Mitch

Today chugs + cabin activity was fun. In High Ropes, I did the zip line (harress on, go on wire, across the lake + back). It was a ton of fun, even though I got a wedgy.

Dear All,   JULY 14 '04

    I definitely have Pinkeye. Both eyes. It stinks. This morning I slamed my *middle* finger in the door. I can't swim because of my Pinkeye. Amanda has it too. She got it at the same time I did. I hate the drops I have to put in to get rid of it. I will be finished with the drops by the time I get home. Yay! *This* *(forgot 'bout this sentence)* morning ~~Lucy Brought~~ Lucy let ~~the~~ the door slam, + it slamed on my finger. It really hurt + is swollen. I put ice on it + it helped.

                                          Jessica

Sam tripped on the flag pole + sprained her ankle. She was on crutches for 2 days. She had it x-rayed at a hospital to find it was a bad sprain. Now she is fine and wears an air cast to help it heal faster. She even danced some tonight. Now pink eye is going around + Darla has it. We have to wash our hands like 50 times a day + Darla 100. We're all being very careful. I have NOT had any sick~~nesses~~/rashes this year!!

Nancy's
Laura

Dear Mom, Dad, ~~Kevin,~~ and Claire and Kelly,
  By the time this arrives I will already be home.
I can't wait to see you. As much as I'm enjoying
camp, I'm ready to come home. I really excited
to tell you about all of my cool experiences. Like
today when I almost died in horseback
riding. I was barebacking, meaning I
   was riding without a saddle when my horse
bucked me off and the horse in front of
me kicked me three or four times in mid air.
My buttox and legs kill. I LOVE YOU, Sean

Dear mom + dad,

Hi! I had a fever 2 day!! But, it turned out I was dehydrated! I'm fine now! It is sooo hot out 2 day!!! Me and Lexi are next 2 eachother on the top! (how we planned.) My bunk is barnard my counselors are Amber, Anna, Rachel, and Chelsea! Love, Olivia

What
I Really
Need...

Mom, please send me a strapless bra. there might be one in my drawer, if not please go to Limited 2 and get me one! ~I'm a 34 I'll pay you back! Please! Thanks!

Carly

To: _____
_____
_____
_____

© 2000 Mary Patricia Deprez dba Dye Mary

Dear Mom

I'm getting really disapointed that I dont have a tennis raket, because all of these kids are playing tennis and I could probley whoop there asse only if I had my teqnis raket. So will you please send me my tennis raket

Thanks
Love Ya
Bye

Sincerly
Ben

Dear Mom and Dad
    Don't send me the
ticket. I want to stay here
for longer I guess I was
just having a bad day.
Now I'm having a great
time I leave for my trip
in an hour Thank you

        Love Alex

P.S. candy please

P.S.S. were starving
we need candy

P.S.S.S. CANDY

send cookies

Dear Family,
today I got your package. It was a
terrible basket. Please send candy. We had a practice
campout, I was good, I met Coleman. I also met
Tomy. I went back climbing, I got hit in
the back of the head with a cricket
paddle. I have a big bump but I am fine. I've
been swimming, canoeing, kayaking, and played soccer.

I am having fun

Love,
Dylan

Dear Mom,
    Sorry for the short letter.
Send Gatorade powder, and keep
sending it. Also a lot of gum.
Use your imagination to send
other stuff I will like. heres
other ideas, BBQ sunflower seeds, my
  Fmg hat, Beef Jerky, Gummy bears,
peach rings, and all the other good
stuff.
    Love ya
    Quinn

Dear Mom + Dad,
       Grant
has his own
gun. it is a black
22. cal ~~~~ semi auto-
matic rifle. I ~~got
to try it first period.
To break the ~~gun in, we
just took turns blasting
it at targets. I have
decided that I don't
wan't a ping-pong
table. I really want
to get a 22. cal
semi atomatic black
rifle.

Dear Mom & Dad,

Camp is Great! I accidently
Forgot to bring a
baseball cap. Can you send
Me one (not cubs) as soon
as Possible, I need one
For the Dunes Trip. Also
Please Don't send any
of the hats in my room
b/c Most of them are
really gay.

P.S.
sox hat if Possible

Love,

SAM

Hi Mom + Dad, What's up. Camp so far is great. How is everything at Home. By the Way I accidently left some small wooden beads on my desk. IF you Find Them can you ship them to me. Thanks

Love you

SAM

Quinn

Dear Mom,
Camps going pretty
good I mabe pillow
fighting and Indian danceing
championships, PLEASE
send money for the
airport and send more FOOD

Love U,
From Quinn

Quinn

Please send more food.
~~th~~ not junk, food like
doritos or something, And
please send the greatfull
Dead cd,

Miss u so much

love, Quinn

BUNK REPLY STATIONERY

Dear, Mom
I need a little more money in t.p.
Account. I was woundering if I could
get a mowhawk at camp PlZ PlZ PlZ?
I sent Beverly 2 notes I had a neckloce and
a bunk buddy and I dollar. Have you told
the family about beverly if not tell them.

P.S. PlZ send me a packages
P.P.S Can I PlZ PlZ PlZ PlZ
get a mowhawk at camp.
P.P.P.S my rash she's are doing
♡ Harry fine.

Dear Betsy,

My mom is horrible at sending good packages (aka, chinese books) and because you sent Karly the MOST ~~Awesome~~ package I was wondering if you could ~~Help~~ (like, do everything except the $) her send one with an Awesome pillow! ~~\\\\\\~~ and umm... "Pickles" in a game like the (candy) Yatze. You did an awesome job.

Please, Please, Please!

♡—

Leah

P.S. will you tell my mom where you got ~~the~~ pillow?

65

Mom-
Everyone in my cabin shaves. Can you please send a razor? And send more book stamps!

THANKS

Love,
Zoey

Dear mom,
  I bought a long
razor at the
Camp store, but it
is disposible so it
won't last long. Please
bring a razor and
shaving cream when you visit me.

Also bring a long sleeve shirt.

to: _____
_____
_____
_____

Dear daddy,

ew! the food is yucky!
I need you to send food
to me. those are choices
*please?!! :-)
• doritos   IM still having fun
• mentos
• oreos
• softchew cookies ← not
• chips   required
• hostess cake thingers :-)

this is how, you wrap the
food   in a box with wrapping
paper, then put a card on top
that says... HAPPY BIRTHDAY
Lauren! then they wont check
for food!
                    love
                    Samantha

68

Dear Mom,

why haven't you sent me a letter?

Everyone else has gotten at least one but I haven't. I am really worried who died? What happen? Is anything wrong? WRITE BACK??

Love,
Meredith

Dear, Family
guess what happened today I sliced
my shin open and I could see the
bone, But I am OK, I am also haveing
a good time, but I miss you

I lost my winde up Flashlight some
where plz send a new ~~won~~ one.

♥ Harry

Dear ~~###~~ Family,
I tryed ~~#####~~ $\underline{2}$ new
foods! I tryed exploding
hamster and chesse omlet!
I only like the chesse
omlets. There so so GOOD!

Love
Zoey

Dear Mom,
guess what? Yesterday my
cabin had lice check,
And at the end I was the
only one without lice!
AGAIN! We did the
shampo and made a
spa day out of it. I am
in sunrise cabin and
my counslers are Kate
S. and Anna
its the best cabin ever!
    I LOVE YOU, Gienet

and   aug. 7. 04

Dear. Mom, Dad, Blake,
    I am having so
much fun. Today
I went   tubing
It was Awesomme
Man! also we saw
a dead snake in
the middle of the
road butt we did not
know if it was dead
so I picked it up
and it was <u>dead</u>.
a   I have to go get
bye   oyster crackers.!
      XOXO love, Biana

76

Dear Daddy,
Today at the petting
zoo at camp the
dogs tried to eat the rabbit
and the kittens cause
they didn't like me
and took my shoes +
I throw the ball
over a kitten &
the kitten ran
and the dog chased
it so the kitten went
thow the fence and
up a tree e so the
counselors had to up stuck
to get the kitten out
of the tree I felt bad
so I went swimming
- KYLA

P.S. MOM, DAD!
Somebody stole my colored
pencils, ~~also~~ stole a kids
scetch book and wriped up
his drawings! Palease send me
more colored pencils!

Never Mind.
we fond the
stuff they stole

A Boyhood Adventure

Dear Mom and Dad,
Just forget about my colored pencils ~~were~~ getting stolen. You see I wrote the letter to you, I went to play kickball I came back and my pencils were missing I wrote the extra part on my letter, sealed it, and then I a found my kid ~~colored the~~ colored pencils.

Love,
Henry

Camp's Fun!

© ZM20-415

Dear Mommy & Daddy
Yesterday me &
my friends jumped
in the pool with
our clothes on It
was really fun!
I also have some
~~good~~ Funny /bad ~~news~~ news
Rachel dumped me
but the funny news
is she's dating her
cousin. Ha
Love, Mikey

MADISON WI 537
24 JUL 2006 PM 4 L

Common Buckeye

Dear Mom and Dad, you said in an e-mail that you haven't gotten any letters from me that doesn't make sense because I sent you like 12. I think I mite have messed up the return addressi Anyway my first session

trip was great and I'm looking

forward to my second session trip. I've been finding a lot

of things in the lake I found two knifes and a bunch of old

glass soda bottles that d either

give people or sell them for pops.

81

Dear mom and dad,
thank you for the stampr
and evelopes. Now I can wright.

LoVe

Mark

p.s. yes I did did slow dance
with a girl named Haley. I
grabbed her hips. I even got her
home Address.

LoVe

Mark

Dear Mom and Dad

Last night we came back from general swim only to find flying ants this big ⊢———⊣ we had to sleep in another cabin, cabin 16 it was a mess   miss you

still haven't found my Mitt

Rose Mary

Dear mom and Dad,

I got back from my trip and it was so-so. The first day was nothing special, just paddling, not much. The dinner was macaroni pasta with sauce and bread with this half awsom garlic sauce. The 1st half of the second day we had like 8 actualy rapids in a row. Then after lunch (which was hotdogs) the river got really wide and steep and we had hard wind blowing in our face so it was like paddeling up stream. That stunk. The dinner was stir frying made rice with this sauce withe Veggies and Juices that was amazing. The next day it rained and it was freezing. That was awful but we only had to canoe a little bit.

Dear Mom & Dad,

The second you left I ran to write a letter to tell you how many friends I made. One kid is playing other kids for $50 in poker. 1 kid lost $10. But don't worry I didn't play. If I did I would play the house.

miss you,
Sam

P.S.
Dad that poker set could have been useful after all.

Dear mom & dad,

I just came from formula "K"
and I got charlie a present
it is a blow up alien thing.
Also this year the counselers aren't
as nice ~~they~~ one of them hates
my ideas all the time but the rest
are nice.

P.S.
Nick, the riflery
teacher from last
year got
fired for inhaling
crack at camp.
He also went to jail.

86

Dear mom and it ti

David ban Two

Hi today I skied around
the lake to day! ⬤ it
was so fun! hi its
Jordan for a fact
david really skied
around the lake

Love
DAVID

Dear Mom and Dad,
    I really miss you.
The first day I cried
because I got homesick.
I missed you guyes,
they made me clean
the table I want to
go HOME

    I just came back
from skits that the
counslers did. I stopped
crying. It got much
more fun. But we
have chores today
I am the scraper,
sweeper, and maid

    I just came back
from breakfast
I'm having more fun
        Love
            Bianca

90

Dear Mom,

TAKE ME

HOME!

From,
Rose
||
A

⭐ **Olivia** ⭐

Date: _____

⭐ Mom, Dad I am
trying to be my self
but noone in my
cabin likes me come ⭐
and pick me up
I hate camp!
call the office
and say you need to
talk to me or come
⭐ and visit I am in the
play it is pocahntis.

_____

_____

WRITE ME!

⭐

★ Olivia

Date: _____

Mommy, Daddy come and get me, Pick me up I am crying I miss you to much to be here come to get me!!!!! PLAESE!!

ME→

I ♥ camp   Gabby→

WRITE ME!

93

Date: _____

Take me home Mommy
Take me home DaDDy
Take me home Mommy
Take me home Daddy
Take me home Mommy
Take me home Daddy
Take me home Mommy
Take me home Daddy
Take me home Mommy
Take me home Daddy
Take me home Mommy
Take me home Daddy
Take me home Mommy

WRiTE ME!

I ♡ U

~~I always~~ I allso
miss you!

Love,

Olivia

Dear Mom and
Dad send me pics.
I miss you when
will I see you!
I cry so much
nothing is fun.

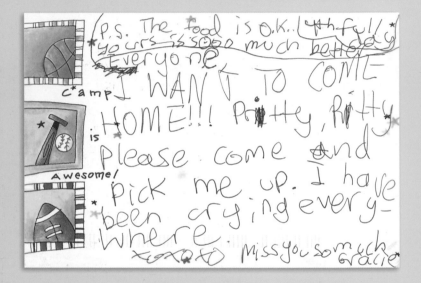

Dear Mommy and Daddy,

I am really really homesick. I know you want me to have fun but I can't! I am sitting on my steps to the cabin crying I HATE IT HERE! the letter before this about me starting to have fun was not true I just wanted you to be happy and proud of me! I am misrable here please come pick me up. I am starting to forget you vocies. I just really really really really really want to come home! I did 5 reallys for the 5 of us. If you want to be mean by keeping me here fine. But DONT sine me up agian I need you to live my life.

Love your Daughter that needs you.
Piper

P.S. Come pick me up or you would be so so sooo mean

97

Dear Mom and dad.
this is how I am all
the time here!

come pick me up.

Love.
Piper

Camp Rocks... ^(Doesn't)

Dear Mom and Dad,

I ■ wrote you this song.

There is only a ~~lttle~~ litle bite of summer

left and I want to spend it with you ~~to~~

three but not here I just want to be with you

I ~~e~~ need to go now just remember thissss

GOOD BYE! GOOD BYE! GOOD BYE!

I love you!

Love, Piper

PS COME PICK ME UP!

Dear mom and dad,
   HURRY!
I haven't unpacked
my stuff yet, I refuse
to. I am histarically
crying! I hate my
life right now! →

I haven't been able to eat
anything (no joking) for
breakfast, lunch or dinner
since I got here. I think
it is because I am depressed.
I already tried to runaway
but they caught me. I just
really want to come home!
       Love, your unhappy
daughter Elizabeth

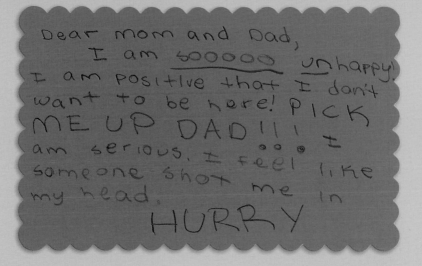

Dear mom and Dad,
    I am sooooo unhappy!
I am positive that I don't
want to be here! PICK
ME UP DAD!!! I
am serious. I feel like
someone shot me in
my head. HURRY

I tried
to runaway
but they caught
me! (seriously)

Dear family,   06/04

Hi, I miss you so much, I really want to come home. how is uncle John in Michigan. Anything new in the house and anything happening at the house or any family members or friends? Did Tali sell her house? Did I get my cell phone yet? How is our family, does Jake still have long hair? Did Jake get better at guitar? Does Jake still point his nails? Is dad less Grumpy. Did I miss anything important at home? How was the fourth of July? Mine stunk, I am writing this letter on the fourth of July. I had a bunch of Depression today, I had so much I prayed to god (Our god the Jewish one) last night. Since there was no synagogue up I prayed at the chapel, it was better than nothing. I have met a lot of friends in case you were wondering. I haven't had a chicken patty yet but their food is amazing. I will actual Eat a full Hot Dog like with the bun, I like milk by itself now, I like the drawing book but there is nothing to draw here. I can't wait to see you guys again. I miss you sooooo much. I don't LIKE camp too much and I don't think I want to come back next year. My counsilers are cool. All of Jakes friends say hi, I talk to all of them. Do you know if we are going to John and Carls house after camp? I NEED TO BE UPDATED ON EVERYTHING!!! camp would be ok if I had a different cabin (different cabin kids). One of the kids from my cabin I knew from home. Make sure Jake brings two guitars, I need to play guitar soon! My counsilers give us guys candy but whenever you get in a while, I takes a while to get some rest around here because no one ever quiets down. hope you got my letters. well I have to go bye.

                                                 love,
                                                 Mitch

P.S. Sorry for writing small and close together

Dear Mom & Dad,   July 4, 2007

You know me, I complain, but once
I get somewhere I usually have fun. This
is not fun. I am not exagerating when
I say this is the worst week of my
life ever. Camp sucks!! Why?
I am homesick, I know kids, but
not well enough to follow them around
every day. Yesterday I went to Jordan
started blubbering like a baby, and said I
want to go home, He said that wasn't
an option I can't take this for much
longer, though. I want you to make
Jordan let me leave!! Please I am
begging you. I am embarassed to
say, I cry every day. This is not a
camp from my dreams, it's the 100th level
of hell. Save me or else I will
get out of here by doing something
stupid. I am not joking. I hate
this stupid camp. I am getting
out of here. Write me. I NEED
MORE STAMPS. Save me!!! I am out of
       Love Zach   stamps

Dear Mom and Dad,

~~Mmmd~~ I'm having a blast at camp, not! It's so borring here, the only fun activities are tether ball, Archery and Nuketem. I miss you tons!

Love
mark

P.s, I hate it here.

Love
mark

DEAR ___Mom & Dad___
CAMP IS ___okay___
I'M ___sorry to say but after___
___2 days I wanna go home everyday.___
___I go in the pool & the chlorine___
___burns my eyes !! then I___
SEE YOU SOON! ___get a migraine___
___Mikey___

P.S. I need
goggles
badly

oppi P-114

Dear Family, 6/24/03
Camp is okay. I
was homesick at the
lake waiting for swim test
and all today I've
been crying mysterionsly
for the beacause I
was so homesick.
Today I talked to Dana
and she made me feel
better. Rachel (my counslor)
went with me. It's rest
period right now. Last
night I threw up
beacause I took
a bite of a
meatball!

Dear Mom and Dad,

I'm kinde having fun. I don't really like the kids in my group some are super annoying and they don't try do to the activities. I'm in koogee 13 and Phil is in K-10 I think? but I guess we are relativly close, I'll try to have more fun. I will also try to ignore the annoying kids in my group.

I will see you soon,
Love
Pat

P.S. Tell dad happy father's day.

Hi mom and Dad
I haVing lots
of fun. I only
get homesick when
I not doing anything
Like eating Dinner
Love,
Patrick

Dear mom, and dad, writing the letter. (It was really Thoughtful.)
Thank you for writing the letter. (It was really Thoughtful.)

I miss you so much. My first time sleeping here, I couldn't sleep.
Are you having a good time? I may not surprise.

I'm having a good time. I love cameing! The latter is cold.
Is your lake cold   see you

From
charlie

Dear Mom,

I really want you to come and visit me. I am crying right now and I really really miss you right now and I want to come home please come and visit. I love you so much. You are the best.

With all my heart,
Brian

Hello mr. & mrs. B.   It's adam

    I really want you to come
and so does Brian. He ~~He~~ is crying
his eyes out and he's just not
the same anymore. Pleas Come

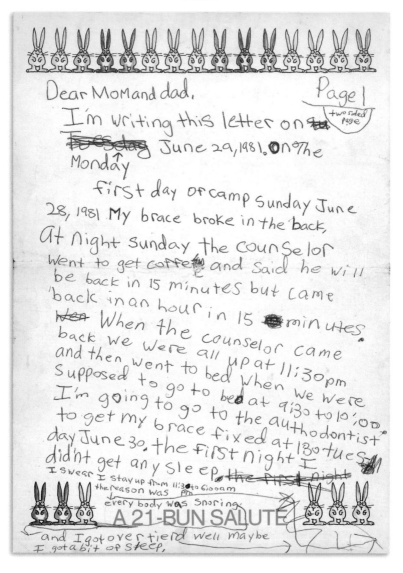

Dear Mom and dad,

Page 1
~~two sided~~ two sided page

I'm writing this letter on ~~the~~

~~Tuesday~~ June 29, 1981. On the

Monday↑

first day of camp Sunday June

28, 1981 My brace broke in the back,

At Night sunday the counselor

went to get ~~coffee~~ and said he will

be back in 15 minutes but came

back in an hour in 15 ~~Hea~~ ⬤ minutes.

When the counselor came

back we were all up at 11;30pm

and then went to bed When we were

supposed to go to bed at 9;30 to 10;00

I'm going to go to the authodontist

to get my brace fixed at 1;30 tues

day June 30, the first night I

didn't get any sleep ~~the first night~~

I swear I stay up from 11;30 to 6;00 am

the reason was pm

every body was snoring.

and I got over tierd well maybe

I gota bit of sleep,

And I probally (won't get to sleep) tonight
Mon. June 29, 81. Every body in
the ~~camp~~ cabin I hate except
(yoo Hoo) Michael ~~and~~ this
kid is always wiseing off to me I want
to kill him. I'm so inbarist
at camp everyone ~~no~~ knows where
everything is and I don't so when
I ask ~~Bu~~ My counselor he dosent
answer. Theres also another
thing -but I won't say. I hate it
but all activeities ~~didn't~~ didn't start
yet they will ~~June Bu~~ June 30
I want to go home but first I
have to wait till June 30. Everything
is bad they won't let me call
you and I cant wait till
this letter reaches you. Josh wrote
in his other letter ~~he~~ that. he likes
it well he told Me to tell you he
and me, Michael, Y and Michael F hate
it so ~~me~~ much continue next
page.

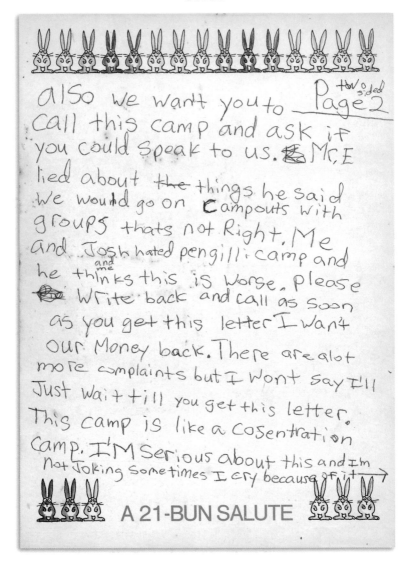

also we want you to <u>Page 2</u> ^{two sided}
call this camp and ask if
you could speak to us. ~~~~ Mr, E
lied about ~~the~~ things he said
we would go on campouts with
groups thats not Right. Me
and Josh hated pengilli camp and
he th^{and}_{me}inks this is worse, please
~~~~ Write back and call as soon
as you get this letter I want
our Money back. There are alot
more complaints but I wont say I'll
Just wait till you get this letter.
This camp is like a Cosentration
camp. I'M Serious about this and Im
not Joking sometimes I cry because of it ⟶

A 21-BUN SALUTE

114

but very little. I want to stay with Josh or call you but they won't let me call or anything. The counselor is nice but is going to wake us up at 6:30 and I didn't get any sleep as I already menchord. The whole lake is seawead I'm not going swimming I want to go to westchester day if we get our money back. Everyone talks at night and snores I cant go to sleep with snoreing trying not to suck my thumb, I want to go home Now, call the office to talk to us, we will get our money to come as soon as you get this message. I cant not go to sleep for 8 weeks all this happened in two days. sorry about all this but I. Just dont like it and please call I'm crying while writing this message.

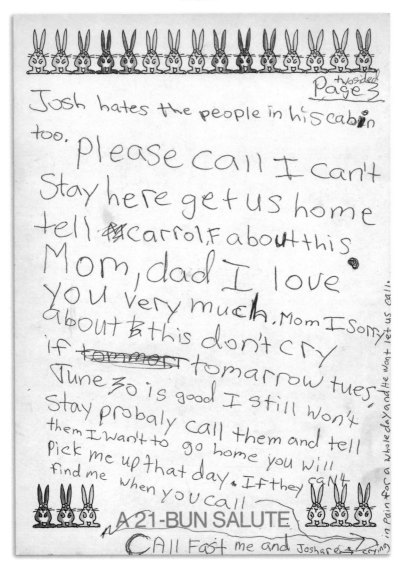

Page 3 twosided

Josh hates the people in his cabin too. PLEASE CALL I can't Stay here get us home tell ~~Mrs~~ carrol,F about this. Mom, dad I love You very much. Mom I sorry about ~~is~~ this don't cry if ~~tormor~~ tomarrow tues, June 30 is good I still won't Stay probaly call them and tell them I want to go home you will Pick me up that day. If they can't find me when you call

A 21-BUN SALUTE

CAll Fast me and Josh are crying

in Pain for a whole day and He wont let us call.

tell them to have me call
you as soon as they see me.
I know you will kill me but
thats whats happening something
somethings are good but hardly any.
Write back and call,

Pick Me up.

I love you very
much michael you was sick at dinner
the counselor woudent let him go to
the bathroom so he threw up, I feel
like Im going to through up
because of worry ness tell
Mr. E about this,
make sure you call and reach us fast.
I bet it make sure you remember

A lot of things are wrong
and we have been crying. The next
pages tell some things that went
wrong skip the lake part I hate
it because of the seaweed but
I hate it anyway but I will like
it a little because the seaweads
going to float away because
they cut it its floating but it will
float away, Mom it's not as
bad as I said but it's pretty bad.
It says I wanted to go home
at first but I will stay, Just call
and ask for me, If they can't find me
Just give me permition to call you.
I don't Really want to come home
but I do. I HATE

A 21-BUN SALUTE

Back

The 2 night was worst than the first
Me, Josh, Michael Y, ~~Michael were~~ were
crying alot I was crying alot the
second day And they wouldeont let me
call you, I hate it so far, ~~the it~~
a little

Call ~~the~~ Me tell them ~~my~~ office
to find me and if they
can't ~~give~~ tell them to give me
Pemishion to call you

Write back
fast also and
tell me how to solve my
Problems in camp.

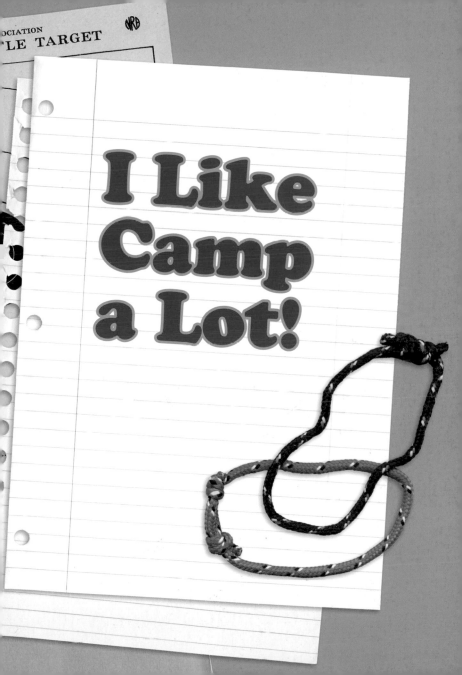

OCIATION
LE TARGET

I Like Camp a Lot!

dear, mom and dad I just lost a tooth! Ψx, I like camp alot. can you send me 5 bucks since I lost a tooth please...

P.S. I am still not homesick

Dear Mom and Dad,   6-26-03

Camp is great! But right now it
is raining very hard so I can't do
anything on my schedule. I met a lot
of new friends and I learnd new
words but not good words. Also one
of my friend came to camp all the
way from Mexico.

From
Sam

Dear ~~XXXXX~~ Mom, and Dad,

I'm in OpTimist _____ Lodge.

(Please put this on any letters, bunk notes, or faxes you send me.)

News from camp: I love camp I'm having fun! I got ur letter, there's no Forbidan cabin, and I diden4 get droped of in a desert!

(signed) RYAN!

Dear Alex,
  I am doing great. Yes my parents are
going away to New York. I did not meet any
cute girls beause they are across the
lake. Yes, I am popular here, I have
made alot of friends here. The N
activities that I picked war Archery, Soccer
Kayaking and Nuke'em, theare really
fun so far. Love you tons too. Mark.

          Love
            Mark

Dear mom and/or Dad,   6/27/08
Camp is so cool! Dad and I had a great
time in portland. I miss you guys. Sadly, I'm
missing my fishing pole. If you see it anywhere
at home, please send it. I can use the camps
for now, but I would like to use my own. Missing
you! Send, send, send!
I told dad that I wanta video camera.
Please ~~wat~~ try to get me one!
And, I left my "Book of Moe"
at our house, so send that, too.

Thanks

Love,
Mason.

Dear Mom,Dad,

Hey!, It's about the middle of camp.
I love it! I went on white flead
and it was aosame! I mawd the lawn there,
and I could do that at home for money,
Send some more letters and care packages
with food. (no candy) pleasel

Love,
nason

Hi Daddy,
        I'm at camp
It's hard, fun, and
all you can eat. But
I'm not gaining weight
cause the hardwork keep
me thin, healthy, and
fit. Really.
                    -Kyla

Dear Family,

Camp is very fun. I learned how to play cricket. I also met Jack and Jacob. My counslers names are kevin and Dylan. The weather is pretty chilly. I don't have any blanckets. For our backpacking trip we are taking an 1½ ferry ride to Manatoo Island. We will spend 2 nights on North Manitoo and 2 nights on S Manitoo with hiking in beetween. we will also canoe the sturgeon river.

P.S. send cookies!!!!! Nobody in our cabin has gotten any yet :(

Love, Dylan

	AM 9:00/ 9:45	AM 9:55/ 10:40	AM 10:50 11:35	
Mon. Wed. Fri.	Biking/ Crafts	Horse Riding/ Golf	Soccer	Lun Rest
Tue. Thur. Sat.	Basketball	Rifle	Base-Ball	Sa

AM 11:45/ 2:00 PM	2:10/ 2:55 PM	3:05/ 3:50 PM	4:00/ 4:45 PM	4:55/ 8:30 PM
ch/ Hour	Archery (bow drawing)	Connoe / OEC (outdoor edication center) (canoe drawing)	swimming (swimmer drawing)	Free Hour — Dinner — After Dinner Game
(up arrow) me	Teunis (tennis racket drawing)	Sailing (sailboat drawing)	Skiing (skier drawing)	(up arrow) Same

131

MIMNEAPOLIS MN 554

19 JUL 2008 PM 11

Dear M,D
I love my
chalez and+
clean my ears
and where
lots of bug spray
Bye,
Louise XOXO XOXO

1st week Tuesday

HEY GUYS,

CAMP is Still great and I Still love You. Oh ya and thanks for telling me your adress for camp Gabby. Right now it's raining. It is rest period now as I'm writing this. Also Yesterday I had My first riflry class. I sent some MY first ever targets. I got 2 Bullseyes.

I'm not trying to be rude but You're taking money out of MY acoun so STOP E-Mailing flease.

"Hi" from camp!

HI guys. Everyday is really fun. on Thursday we went on our canoe down the Jordan. Also, I'm taking a class on rifelry. I might be in a bout race called the Riccotta. Love you see you soon.

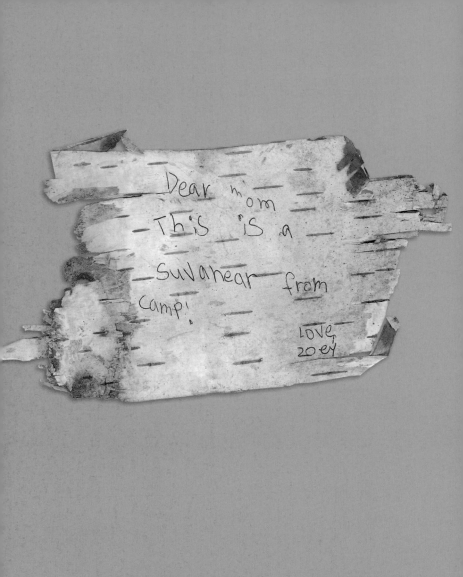

Dear mom
This is a
Suvanear from
camp!
love,
Zoey

136

Dear mom and

I'm having a great time
are you having a great time,
yesterday night
movie night we had
saw Rocky IV and we
was about a guy and in
rocky and he was a good named

boxer and there was another
really strong box that
killed and ther boxer
and than Rocky beat
the other boxer.

love,
Jeremy

P.s Please send another
package.

Dear Mom & Dad
    I just got back from the trip! It was not bad, ~~it~~ it didn't suck but it was good and fun. Unfortunately there ~~were~~ sometimes ~~where~~ I did really stupid things And the counsulers got pissed. And ~~there~~ were sometimes ~~that~~ when I did smart things and the counselers were happy ~~with me~~. It was really tire jing, but I ~~know~~ now have bigger muscles. ~~boy~~ I liked the trip alot.
      (On the ~~~~ back a map of
         our trip)

   These are some fun things I did —
    ① Camped on remote islands
    ② Jumped of the Esex bridge
    ③ Saw sweet lookin waterfalls

   These are some things that made me proud (I might over react)
    ① Canoed ~~~~ untill my fingers bleeded
    ② carried a 50lbs duleath Pack on a ragh trail for a mile

       Love ya
       Bye
       Sincerly
       Ben
               (over)

Manitou Lake

wat ions Scatts good

Manitou stretch

Esox Lake

Ssa Lake

ONtario

Δ = Camp ground
--- = portage
— = Canoe trail
≈ = 2 hi gh
⊢ = highway

Scale

⊢—⊢—⊢—⊢—⊢
10 miles

Dear Mom

I'm having a great time at camp I have tons of friends and the counselors are nice. Some kids have discmen so could you sent my CD I ordered.... Thanks.

Oh and can you please also send some candy, because we gamble for candy. Oh and not to be rude or anything but the following candy would be the best.

- One bag of Fun size crunch bars
- 3 smint boxs.
- A bag of blow pops.

Thanks
Love ya
Bye
Sincerly
Ben

Dear Mom and Dad and Deb,

I'm having a real good up here, yesterday which was Monday, ~~and~~ we ~~to~~ had special day and we had a pow wow (where people have different things to do, and challenge other people who can do it too. I chalenged someone to a keep talking! contest and I won.

Dear Family

Camp is so
Much fun!! I got
ur package the
day after I sent
the letter. I ♡
You People
so Much

Love
Meredith

142

Dear Mom & abba

I made the team
for soccer. Also I'm making
a spatula for you in black-
smithing and I got a new record
for rifery. Today is specialty
day and earth day. I love
camp. I'll give you an example.
Think of the best thing you can.
multiply it by 1000. Thats camp
I love you guys. Say hi to
rahm + tai.

love,
Noah

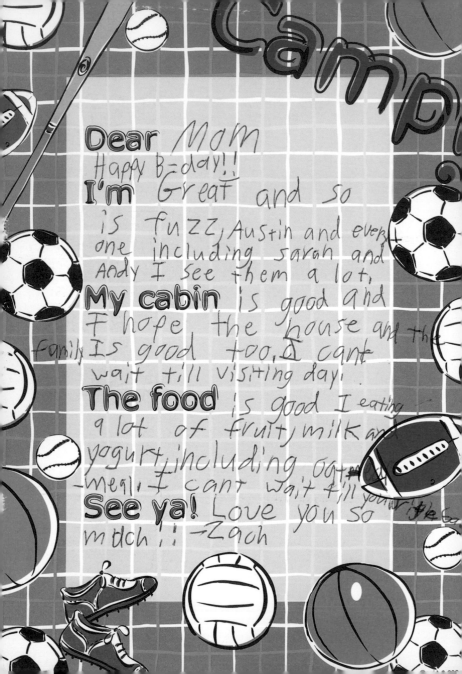

Dear Mom
Happy B-day!!
I'm Great and so
is fuzz, Austin and every
one including sarah and
Andy I see them a lot.
My cabin is good and
I hope the house and the
family Is good too. I cant
wait till visiting day.
The food is good I eating
a lot of fruit, milk and
yogurt, including oat-
-meal. I cant wait till your
See ya! Love you so
much!! →Zach

Dear Mom and Dad,   7/11/07

Today is my second to last day of camp.
I've had so much fun here. I'll definently coming
~~I~~ next year for four weeks. We've already gone to
Sleeping Bear ~~Dunes~~ Dunes. I was alot of fun!
We went dune jumping, swam in lake Michigan,
and hiked a 450 ft. dune and ran down. My favorite
meal will be tonight, we're having ribs and ~~banquiet~~ banquiet.
Banquiet ~~is~~ is where counselors buy a ton of candy
and you eat it. My counselors are really cool. we've
had a lot of fun together. our "rotent" problem
has settled down. I've been playing my guitar.
The next time you'll hear from me will be
Friday from John's lake house.

                           Love,
                           Nicholas

P.S.S. I have presents for all of   P.S. The Brownies ~~were~~ were
you so don't open ~~my~~ big bag.   dilisiouseveryone liked them.

Dear Dad + Mom,
   Can I please
stay for 2 ~~3~~ weeks
more? Since you
didn't answer the
phone, Gaby's mom
said it was OK, so
Gaby gets to stay 2 more
weeks. If u say "no",
U'll get this letter
when I'm back
    I ♥ u? →
    Love Meredith ♥

P.S. MaryJane has been trying to call You. I'll be Very Sad if I can't stay. ~~Kittens~~ Please Please Please▽.

I Love u

Love,
Meredith♡

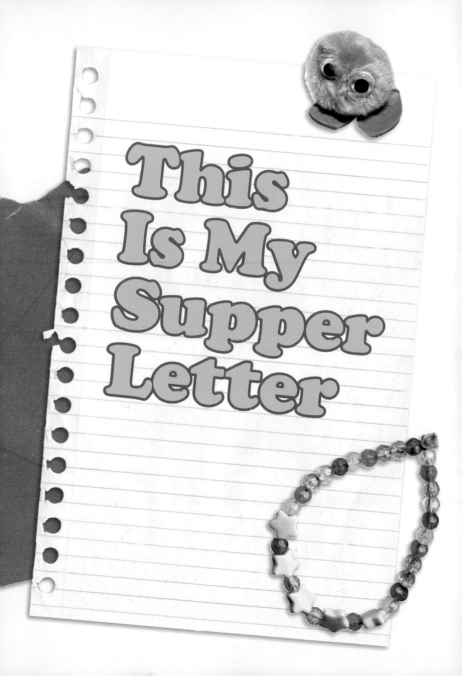

This Is My Supper Letter

Dear, Mom, Dad, and the
hole family
How are you? I had
to stay in the Infurmury
because my glands were
sore. My letter is short
but this is my supper letter.
Love, Deb

Dear, Mom, Dad, Terri, and Buffy—
Tuesday was specail day.
Monday night a u f o was
spotted. It was a space
ship. That night I was
crying because I thought
it was real — This is my supper
letter. Love,
Deb

150

Dear Mom,
 Will you send a pen
up. This is a supper letter.
                         Love,
                         Deb

Dear Mom & Dad

I'm having fun at camp
this letter is a meal ticket
so instead of telling you
what's going on, I'm gonna
write you pointless crap

I like to eat, eat, eat
apples and bananas

I like to eat, eat, eat,
apples and bananas

~~I like to eat~~

Sincerely
    Love Forever

Camp

Dear MoM and Dad
I'm gleat

My cabin good.

The food gleat

See ya! David

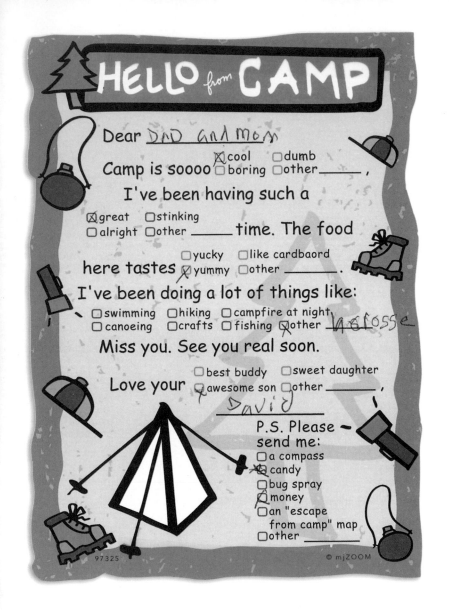

HELLO *from* CAMP

Dear <u>DAD AND MOM</u>

Camp is soooo ☒cool ☐dumb
☐boring ☐other _____ ,

I've been having such a

☒great ☐stinking
☐alright ☐other _____ time. The food

here tastes ☐yucky ☐like cardbaord
☒yummy ☐other _____ .

I've been doing a lot of things like:

☐swimming ☐hiking ☐campfire at night
☐canoeing ☐crafts ☐fishing ☒other <u>lagrosse</u>

Miss you. See you real soon.

Love your ☐best buddy ☐sweet daughter
☒awesome son ☐other _____ ,

<u>David</u>

P.S. Please
send me:
☐a compass
☒candy
☐bug spray
☒money
☐an "escape
from camp" map
☐other _____

97325   © mjZOOM

154

Dear Mom + Dad,

This isn't my long letter but I had to write it for supper. they didn't believe I wrote it for lunch.
Love
Jami

Dear Everyone,

I just have to write on this so they know I sent a letter home! Have a great time!

Love
Zoey

Dear Mom
and Dad I
miss you the
food here is
oK yours is
better Love
Louise

Camp News
from Jack

dear parents,
I am in a big rush
everything is great
miss ya!

love,
Jack

P.S. Thank You

First, my wonderful family: Bianca, thank you for letting me find humor in your homesickness . . . and for giving camp another go this year and loving it. Thank you also for helping me read through thousands of camp letters and laughing with me at all the best bits. And thanks for learning so beautifully at a young age how to laugh at yourself (in our house, a critical survival skill).

Blake, thank you for listening to me read and re-read hundreds of camp letters aloud. And for sometimes even pretending that you'd never heard them before. Thanks for your quiet nods of approval and that sweet sparkle of laughter in your eyes.

Mark, thank you for your constant pride, enthusiasm, and counsel and for loving the idea of this book. Thank you for encouraging me to submit the concept to New York literary agents extraordinaire David Kuhn and Billy Kingsland. Thank you for bursting with excitement when we got the news the book was sold and for telling everyone you could find who would listen. Your proud-husband-love has meant the world to me.

Billy Kingsland and David Kuhn of Kuhn Projects, thank you for visualizing this book from the get-go. You embraced this project fully and found the best publisher around—Abrams Image.

Rebecca Kaplan, the sweetest and most enthusiastic editor on the planet, thank you for working with me tirelessly to get the book finished. Danielle Young, our designer, thank you for your wonderful energy and ideas. You both—and the entire Abrams Image team—are the best of the best.

And thank you to the rest of my family—Linda, Elliot, David, Terry, Ralph, Joan, Sal, Dolores, Elise, Gary, Linda, Ed, Dolores S., Pat, Jayne, Tori, Sam, Alex, Rachel, Jeremy, Lily, Louis, and Julia. You have all been so supportive and engaged.

Thanks to so many of my friends who read, critiqued, listened and laughed: Laura Born, Mimi Brault, Bebe Burlingame, Karen Conter, Tricia Cook, Lorin Costolo, Christy Coughlin, Patricia DePoli, Robbie Deveney, Barb Dunlap, Anne-Marie Farley, Sky Geyer, Linda Goldman (my sister), Sheila Kennedy, Marjie Killeen, Janet and Sara Kupper, Emily and Lauren Levy, Valerie Maragos, Janet Olsen, Sandy O'Malley, Peggy Salamon, Cheryl Scherer, Jennie Tashima, Nora Weir, and Pete Wentz. And thanks to so many other friends who emailed my need for camp letters to family and friends around the country.

Thank you to all of the camp directors nationwide who posted my query for letters, and to the American Camping Association. A special thanks to Steve Cole, Gary Forster, Dayna Hardin, Kim Kiser, Jamie Lake, Bruce Netherwood, Chris Pallatto, Melinda Pearce, Steve Purdum, and Scott Weinstein. Thank you also to Susan Noyes and the entire *Make It Better* team, Sally Higginson and Betsy Brint of *Walking on Air*, and Roberta Rubin of the Book Stall.

A big thanks to everyone who sent me their wonderful family camp letters. I received more than three thousand gems from across the country. And to all of the campers . . . thanks for taking loads of stationery and stamps with you to summer camp . . . and for writing home often.

Finally, a shout out to my mom who gave me so many gifts I'm forever thankful for—including humor, love, and constant support. She would be laughing the loudest.

Editor: Rebecca Kaplan
Designer: Danielle Young
Production Manager: Jacquie Poirier

Cataloging-in-Publication Data has been applied for and
may be obtained from the Library of Congress.

ISBN 978–0–8109–8295–6

Printed and bound in China
10 9 8 7 6 5 4 3 2 1

Abrams Image books are available at special discounts
when purchased in quantity for premiums and promotions
as well as fundraising or educational use. Special editions
can also be created to specification. For details, contact
specialmarkets@abramsbooks.com, or the address below.

THE ART OF BOOKS SINCE 1949
115 West 18th Street
New York, NY 10011
www.abramsbooks.com